Report of Committee on Style, Drafting, Transition and Submission on legislative--unicameral and bicameral - Primary Source Edition

Anonymous, Montana. Constitutional Convention (1971-1972). Legislative Committee

BE IT PROPOSED BY THE LEGISLATIVE COMMITTEE:

That there be a new Article on the Legislature to read as follows:

ARTICLE V

THE LEGISLATURE

Section 1. POWER AND STRUCTURE. The legislative power is vested in a legislature of one chamber whose members are designated senators. The people reserve to themselves the powers of initiative and referendum.

Section 2. SIZE. The number of senators shall be provided by law, but it shall not be smaller than 100 nor larger than 105.

Section 3. ELECTION AND TERMS. A senator shall be elected for a term of four years to begin on a date provided by law. One-half of the senators shall be elected every two years.

Section 4. QUALIFICATIONS. A candidate shall be a resident of the state for at least one year next preceding the general election. For six months next preceding the general election, he shall be a resident of the county if it contains one or more districts or of the district if it contains all or parts of more than one county.

Section 5. COMPENSATION. (1) Each senator shall receive compensation for his services and allowances provided by law. No legislature may fix its own compensation.

(2) The legislature shall create a salary commission to recommend compensation for the judiciary and elected members of the legislative and executive departments.

Section 6. SESSIONS. The legislature shall be a

continuous body for two-year periods beginning when newly elected senators take office. Any business, bill, or resolution pending at adjournment of a session shall carry over with the same status to any other session of the legislature during the biennium. The legislature shall meet at least once a year in regular sessions of not more than 60 legislative days. Any legislature may increase the limit on the length of any subsequent session. The legislature may be convened in special sessions by the governor or at the written request of a majority of the senators.

Section 7. VACANCIES. A vacancy in the legislature shall be filled by special election for the unexpired term unless otherwise provided by law.

Section 8. IMMUNITY. A senator is privileged from arrest during attendance at sessions of the legislature and in going to and returning therefrom, unless apprehended in the commission of a felony or a breach of the peace He shall not be questioned in any other place for any speech or debate in the legislature.

Section 9. DISQUALIFICATION. During the term for which he is elected, a senator shall not hold any civil federal, state, county, or municipal office. This prohibition does not apply to a notary public or a member of the militia

Section 10. ORGANIZATION AND PROCEDURE. (1) The legislature shall judge the election and qualifications of senators. It may vest in the courts the power to try and determine contested elections It shall choose it officers from among its members, keep a journal, and make rules for its proceedings. It may expel or punish a senator for good cause shown with the concurrence of two-thirds of all the senators.

(2) A majority of the senators constitutes a quorum. A smaller number may adjourn from day to day and compel attendance of absent members.

(3) The sessions of the legislature and of the committee of the whole, all committee meetings, and all hearings shall be open to the public.

(4) The legislature may establish a legislative council and other interim committees.

Section 11. BILLS. (1) A law shall be passed by bill which shall not be so altered or amended on its passage through the legislature as to change its original purpose. No bill shall become law except by a vote of the majority of all senators present.

(2) Every vote of each senator on each substantive question in the legislature, in any committee, or in committee of the whole shall be recorded and made public. On final passage, the vote shall be taken by ayes and noes and the names entered on the journal.

(3) Each bill, except general appropriation bills and bills for the codification and general revision of the laws, shall contain only one subject, clearly expressed in its title. If any subject is embraced in any act and is not expressed in the title, only so much of the act not so expressed is void.

(4) A general appropriation bill shall contain only appropriations for the ordinary expenses of the legislative, executive, and judicial departments, for interest on the public debt, and for public schools. Every other appropriation shall be made by a separate bill containing but one subject.

(5) No appropriation shall be made for religious, charitable,

industrial, educational, or benevolent purposes to any private individual, private association, or private corporation not under control of the state.

(6) A law may be challenged on the ground of noncompliance with this section only within two years after its effective date.

Section 12. LOCAL AND SPECIAL LEGISLATION. The legislature shall not pass a special or local act when a general act is, or can be made, applicable.

Section 13. IMPEACHMENT. (1) The governor, executive officers, heads of state departments, judicial officers, and such other officers as may be made subject to impeachment by law shall be removed from office upon conviction of impeachment. Other proceedings for removal from public office for cause may be provided by law.

(2) The legislature shall provide for the manner, procedure, and causes for removal by impeachment and shall provide for a tribunal.

(3) Impeachment can be brought only by a two-thirds vote of the legislature. The tribunal hearing the charges shall convict for impeachment only by a vote of two-thirds or more of its members.

(4) Conviction shall extend only to removal from office, but the party, whether convicted or acquitted, shall also be liable to prosecution according to law.

Section 14. DISTRICTING AND APPORTIONMENT. (1) For the purpose of election, the state shall be divided into as many districts as there are senators. Each district shall consist of compact and contiguous territory. All districts shall be as nearly equal in population as is practicable.

(2) In the legislative session following ratification of this constitution and thereafter in each session preceding each federal population census, a commission of five citizens, none of whom may be public officials, shall be selected to prepare a plan for redistricting and reapportioning the state into legislative and congressional districts. The majority and minority leaders of the legislature shall each select two commissioners Within 20 days after their designation, the four commissioners shall select the fifth member, who shall serve as chairman of the commission. If the four members fail to select the fifth member within the time provided, a majority of the supreme court shall select him.

(3) The commission shall submit its plan to the legislature at the first regular session after its appointment or after the census figures are available. Within 30 days after submission, the legislature shall return the plan to the commission with its recommendations. Within 30 days thereafter, the commission shall file its final plan with the secretary of state and it shall become law. The commission is then dissolved.

Section 15. REFERENDUM OF UNICAMERAL LEGISLATURE. (1) In 1980 the secretary of state shall place upon the ballot at the general election the question: "Shall the unicameral legislature form be continued?"

(2) If a majority of the qualified electors voting on the question answer in the affirmative, the form shall be continued, and this section shall be of no further effect.

(3) If a majority of the qualified electors voting on the question answer in the negative, Article ____ of this Constitution is amended by deleting sections 1, 2, 3, 10, 13, and

14, and inserting in lieu thereof the following:

(a) "Section 1. POWER AND STRUCTURE. The legislative power is vested in a legislature consisting of a senate and a house of representatives. The people reserve to themselves the powers of initiative and referendum."

(b) "Section 2. SIZE. The size of the legislature shall be provided by law, but the senate shall not have more than 53 or fewer than 50 members and the house shall not have more than 106 or fewer than 100 members."

(c) "Section 3. ELECTION AND TERMS. A member of the house of representatives shall be elected for a term of two years and a member of the senate for a term of four years, each to begin on a date provided by law. One-half of the senators shall be elected every two years."

(d) "Section 10. ORGANIZATION AND PROCEDURE. (1) Each house shall judge the election and qualifications of its members. It may by law vest in the courts the power to try and determine contested elections. Each house shall choose its officers from among its members, keep a journal, and make rules for its proceedings. Each house may expel or punish a member for good cause shown with the concurrence of two-thirds of all its members.

"(2) A majority of each house constitutes a quorum. A smaller number may adjourn from day to day and compel attendance of absent members.

"(3) The sessions of the legislature and of the committee of the whole, all committee meetings, and all hearings shall be open to the public.

"(4) The legislature may establish a legislative council and other interim committees.

"(5) Neither house shall, without the consent of the other, adjourn or recess for more than three days or to any place other than that in which the two houses are sitting."

(e) "Section 13. IMPEACHMENT. (1) The governor, executive officers, heads of state departments, judicial officers, and such other officers as may be made subject by law shall be removed from office upon conviction of impeachment. Other proceedings for removal from public office for cause may be provided by law.

"(2) The legislature shall provide for the manner, procedure and causes for removal by impeachment and may select the senate as tribunal.

"(3) Impeachment shall be brought only by a two-thirds vote of the house. The tribunal hearing the charges shall convict for impeachment only by a vote of two-thirds or more of its members.

"(4) Conviction shall extend only to removal from office, but the party, whether convicted or acquitted, shall also be liable to prosecution according to law."

(f) "Section 14. DISTRICTING AND APPORTIONMENT. (1) The state shall be divided into as many districts as there are members of the house, and each district shall elect one representative. Each senate district shall be composed of two adjoining house districts, and shall elect one senator. Each district shall consist of compact and contiguous territory. All districts shall be as nearly equal in population as is practicable.

"(2) In the legislative session following this amendment and thereafter in each session preceding each federal population census, a commission of five citizens, none of whom may be public officials, shall be selected to prepare a plan for redistricting and reapportioning the state into legislative and congressional districts. The majority and minority leaders of each house shall each designate one commissioner. Within 20 days after their designation, the four commissioners shall select the fifth member, who shall serve as chairman of the commission. If the four members fail to select the fifth member within the time provided, a majority of the supreme court shall select him.

"(3) The commission shall submit its plan to the legislature at the first regular session after its appointment or after the census figures are available. Within 30 days after submission, the legislature shall return the plan to the commission with its recommendations. Within 30 days thereafter, the commission shall file its final plan with the secretary of state and it shall become law. The commission is then dissolved."

(4) The members of the unicameral legislature shall remain in office and their authority to act shall continue until the members of a bicameral body are elected and qualified.

(5) The Senate chamber existing upon the date of adoption of this Article shall remain intact until the election provided for in this section has determined whether the unicameral legislature is to continue.

(6) When the provisions of this section have been carried out, it shall be of no further effect

Section 16. PROHIBITED PAYMENTS. Except for interest on the public debt, no money shall be paid out of the treasury unless upon an appropriation made by law and a warrant drawn by the proper officer in pursuance thereof.

Section 17. CODE OF ETHICS. The legislature shall provide a code of ethics prohibiting conflict between public duty and private interest for senators and all state and local officers and employees.

BE IT PROPOSED BY THE LEGISLATIVE COMMITTEE:

That there be a new Article on the Legislature to read as follows:

ARTICLE V

THE LEGISLATURE

Section 1. POWER AND STRUCTURE. The legislative power of the state is vested in the a legislature, consisting of one chamber whose members are designated senators. The people reserve to themselves the powers of initiative and referendum.

Section 2. SIZE. The number of senators shall be prescribed provided by law, but there it shall not be not less smaller than 100 members nor more larger than 105.

Section 3. ELECTION AND TERMS OF MEMBERS. A senator shall be elected for a term of four years to begin on a date provided by law. One-half of the senators shall be elected every two years. A senator's term shall begin on a date provided by law.

Section 4. QUALIFICATIONS. A candidate for the legislature shall be a resident of the state for at least one year next preceding the general election. For six months prior to next preceding the general election, he must shall be a resident of the county which if it contains one or more districts, and where a or of the district if it consists contains all or parts of more than one county, he must reside within that district.

Section 5 COMPENSATION (1) Each member of the legislature senator shall receive compensation for his services and allowances as may be prescribed provided by law No legislature may fix its own compensation.

(2) The legislature shall create ~~A~~ a salary commission ~~shall be created by the legislature~~ to recommend compensation for the judiciary and elected members of the legislative~~,~~ and executive~~, and judicial compensation,~~ departments.

Section 6. SESSIONS. The legislature shall be a continuous body for two-year periods beginning ~~on the date~~ when newly elected ~~members~~ senators take office. Any business, bill, or resolution pending at adjournment of a session shall carry over with the same status to any ~~further~~ other session of the legislature during the biennium. The legislature shall meet at least once a year in regular sessions of not more than 60 legislative days ~~or less~~. Any legislature may increase the limit on the length of any subsequent session. The legislature may be convened in special sessions by the governor or at the written request of a majority of the ~~members~~ senators.

Section 7. VACANCIES. A vacancy in the legislature shall be filled by special election for the unexpired term unless otherwise provided by law.

Section 8. IMMUNITY. ~~The members of the legislature shall, in all cases, except felony and breach of the peace, be privileged from arrest during their attendance at the sessions of the legislature, and in going to and returning from the same, and for any speech or debate in the legislature, they shall not be questioned in any other place.~~ A senator is privileged from arrest during attendance at sessions of the legislature and in going to and returning therefrom, unless apprehended in the commission of a felony or a breach of the peace. He shall not be questioned in any other place for any speech or debate in the legislature.

Section 9. DISQUALIFICATION. ~~No-senator-or-representative-shall,-during-the-term-for-which-he-shall-have-been elected,-be-appointed-to-any-civil-office-under-the-state;-and-no member-of-congress,-or-other-person-holding-an-office -(except-notary-public,-or-in-the-militia)-under-the-United States-or-this-state,-shall-be-a-member-of-either-house during-his-continuance-in-office;~~ During the term for which he is elected, a senator shall not hold any civil federal, state, county, or municipal office. This prohibition does not apply to a notary public or a member of the militia.

Section 10. ORGANIZATION AND PROCEDURE. (1) The legislature shall judge the election and qualifications of ~~its-members~~ senators. ~~and~~ It may ~~by-law~~ vest in the courts the ~~trial-and-determination-of~~ power to try and determine contested elections ~~of-its-members~~. It shall choose its officers from among its members~~;~~, keep a journal~~;~~, and make rules for its proceedings~~;~~ ~~and~~ It may expel or punish a ~~member~~ senator for good cause shown with the concurrence of two-thirds of all ~~its-members~~ the senators.

(2) A majority of the ~~membership-of-the-legislature~~ senators constitutes a quorum ~~to-do-business~~. A smaller number may adjourn from day to day and compel attendance of absent members.

(3) The sessions of the legislature~~,~~ and of the committee of the whole, ~~and~~ all committee meetings, and all hearings shall be open to the public.

(4) ~~There-may-be-a-legislative-council-and~~ The legislature may establish a legislative council and other interim

committees.

Section 11. BILLS. (1) A law shall be passed by bill~~, and a bill~~ which shall not be so altered or amended on its passage through the legislature as to change its original purpose. No bill shall become law except by a vote of the majority of all senators present.

(2) ~~The-vote-of-each-member-of-the-legislature and-its-committees-on-any-substantive-question-shall-be recorded-and-made-public.~~ Every vote of each senator on each substantive question in the legislature, in any committee, or in committee of the whole shall be recorded and made public.

(3) ~~No-bill-shall-become-law-except-by-a-vote-of the-majority-of-all-members-present, and o~~On final passage, the vote shall be taken by ayes and noes and the names entered on the journal.

~~(4)~~ (3) Each bill, except general appropriation bills~~,~~ and bills for the codification and general revision of the laws, shall contain only one subject, ~~which-shall-be~~ clearly expressed in its title~~, but i~~. If any subject ~~shall-be~~ is embraced in any act ~~which-shall~~ and is not be expressed in the title, ~~such-act-shall-be-void~~ only ~~as-to~~ so much ~~thereof-as-shall~~ of the act not be so expressed is void. ~~A-law-may-be-challenged-on-the-grounds-of-non-compliance with-this-section-within-two-years-after-its-effective-date but-not-after-that-period.~~

~~(5)~~ (4) A ~~G~~general appropriation bill~~s~~ shall contain only appropriations for the ordinary expenses of the legislative, executive, and judicial departments ~~of-the-state~~, for interest on the public debt, and for public schools.

~~All~~ Every other appropriations shall be made by a separate bill~~s,~~ ~~each~~ containing but one subject.

~~(6)~~ (5) No appropriation shall be made for religious, charitable, industrial, educational, or benevolent purposes to any private individual, private association, or private corporation not under control of the state.

(6) A law may be challenged on the ground of non-compliance with this section only within two years after its effective date.

Section 12. LOCAL AND SPECIAL LEGISLATION The legislature ~~may~~ shall not pass a special or local act when a general act is, or can be made, applicable

Section 13. IMPEACHMENT. (1) The governor, executive officers, heads of state departments, judicial officers, and such other officers as may be made subject to impeachment by law ~~may~~ shall be removed from office upon conviction of impeachment. Other proceedings for removal from public office for cause may be provided by law.

(2) The legislature shall provide for the manner, procedure, and causes for removal by impeachment and shall provide for a tribunal.

(3) Impeachment can be brought only by a two-thirds vote of the ~~senate~~ legislature. The tribunal hearing the charges shall convict ~~and no conviction~~ for impeachment ~~shall-be-made-except~~ only by a vote of two-thirds or more of ~~the~~ its members ~~of-the-tribunal-hearing-the-charges~~.

(4) ~~Such c~~Conviction shall ~~only~~ extend only to removal from office, but the party, whether convicted or acquitted, shall also be liable to prosecution according to law.

Section 14. DISTRICTING AND APPORTIONMENT. (1) For the purpose of ~~electing-members-of-the-legislature~~, election the state shall be divided into as many districts as there ~~shall-be-members-of-the-legislature~~ are senators. Each ~~legislative~~ district shall consist of compact and contiguous territory. ~~and~~ All districts shall be ~~so~~ as nearly equal in population as is practicable.

(2) In the legislative session following ratification of this constitution and thereafter in ~~the~~ each session preceding each federal population census ~~made-by-the authority-of-the-United-States,~~ a ~~committee~~ commission of five citizens, none of whom may be public officials, shall be ~~designated~~ selected to ~~draft~~ prepare a plan for redistricting and reapportioning the state into legislative and congressional districts. The majority and minority leaders of the legislature shall each ~~designate~~ select two commissioners. ~~The-four-commissioners,~~ ~~w~~Within 20 days after their designation, the four commissioners shall select the fifth member, who shall serve as chairman of the commission. If the four members fail to select the fifth member within the time provided ~~prescribed~~, a majority of the supreme court shall ~~appoint-the-chairman~~ select him.

(3) The ~~appointed~~ commission shall ~~draw-up-a-plan-for reapportioning-and-redistricting-legislative-and-congressional districts-and~~ submit ~~this~~ its plan to the legislature at the first regular session after ~~ratification-of-this constitution~~ its appointment or after the census figures are available. Within ~~(30)~~ ~~thirty~~ days after ~~the~~ submission, ~~to it~~ the legislature shall return the plan to the commission with its recommendations. ~~for-change-and-the-commission~~

~~shall~~ wWithin ~~(30) thirty~~ days thereafter, the commission shall file ~~with-the-Secretary-of-State~~ its final plan with the secretary of state and ~~the-same~~ it shall become law. ~~After-enactment-of-a-valid-plan-this~~ The commission ~~shall-be~~ is then dissolved.

Section 15. REFERENDUM OF UNICAMERAL LEGISLATURE. (1) In 1980 the secretary of state shall place upon the ballot at the ~~next-following~~ general election the question: "Shall the unicameral legislature form be continued?"

(2) If a majority of the qualified electors voting on the question answer in the affirmative, the form shall be continued, and this section shall be of no further effect.

(3) If a majority of the qualified electors voting on the question answer in the negative, ~~the-provisions-of Section-1,-"POWER-AND-STRUCTURE",-Section-2,-"SIZE",-Section 3,-"ELECTION-AND-TERMS-OF-MEMBERS",-Section-10,-"ORGANIZATION AND-PROCEDURE",-Section-14,-"IMPEACHMENT",-and-Section-15, "DISTRICTING-AND-APPORTIONMENT"-as-set-forth-in-the-bicameral legislative-proposal-shall-be-substituted-for-Sections-1, 2,-3,-10,-14-and-15-of-this-unicameral-article-and-be controlling-upon-the-composition-of-future-legislative-assemblies~~. Article ____ of this Constitution is amended by deleting sections 1, 2, 3, 10, 13, and 14, and inserting in lieu thereof the following:

(a) "Section 1. POWER AND STRUCTURE. The legislative power is vested in a legislature consisting of a senate and a house of representatives. The people reserve to themselves the powers of initiative and referendum."

(b) "Section 2. SIZE. The size of the legislature shall

be provided by law, but the senate shall not have more than 53 or fewer than 50 members and the house shall not have more than 106 or fewer than 100 members."

(c) "Section 3. ELECTION AND TERMS. A member of the house of representatives shall be elected for a term of two years and a member of the senate for a term of four years, each to begin on a date provided by law. One-half of the senators shall be elected every two years."

(d) "Section 10. ORGANIZATION AND PROCEDURE. (1) Each house shall judge the election and qualifications of its members. It may by law vest in the courts the power to try and determine contested elections. Each house shall choose its officers from among its members, keep a journal, and make rules for its proceedings. Each house may expel or punish a member for good cause shown with the concurrence of two-thirds of all its members.

"(2) A majority of each house constitutes a quorum. A smaller number may adjourn from day to day and compel attendance of absent members.

"(3) The sessions of the legislature and of the committee of the whole, all committee meetings, and all hearings shall be open to the public.

"(4) The legislature may establish a legislative council and other interim committees.

"(5) Neither house shall, without the consent of the other, adjourn or recess for more than three days or to any place other than that in which the two houses are sitting."

(e) "Section 13. IMPEACHMENT. (1) The governor, executive officers, heads of state departments, judicial officers, and such other officers as may be made subject by law shall be removed from office upon conviction of impeachment.

Other proceedings for removal from public office for cause may be provided by law.

"(2) The legislature shall provide for the manner, procedure, and causes for removal by impeachment and may select the senate as tribunal.

"(3) Impeachment shall be brought only by a two-thirds vote of the house. The tribunal hearing the charges shall convict for impeachment only by a vote of two-thirds or more of its members.

"(4) Conviction shall extend only to removal from office, but the party, whether convicted or acquitted, shall also be liable to prosecution according to law."

(f) "Section 14. DISTRICTING AND APPORTIONMENT. (1) The state shall be divided into as many districts as there are members of the house, and each district shall elect one representative. Each senate district shall be composed of two adjoining house districts, and shall elect one senator. Each district shall consist of compact and contiguous territory. All districts shall be as nearly equal in population as is practicable.

"(2) In the legislative session following this amendment and thereafter in each session preceding each federal population census, a commission of five citizens, none of whom may be public officials, shall be selected to prepare a plan for redistricting and reapportioning the state into legislative and congressional districts. The majority and minority leaders of each house shall each designate one commissioner. Within 20 days after their designation, the four commissioners shall select the fifth member, who shall serve as chairman of the commission. If the four members fail to select the fifth member within the time provided, a majority of the supreme court shall select him

"(3) The commission shall submit its plan to the legislature at the first regular session after its appointment or after the census figures are available. Within 30 days after submission, the legislature shall return the plan to the commission with its recommendations. Within 30 days thereafter, the commission shall file its final plan with the secretary of state and it shall become law. The commission is then dissolved."

(4) The members of the unicameral legislature shall remain in office and their authority to act shall continue until ~~their successors-to~~ the members of a bicameral body ~~can-be~~ are elected and qualified.

(5) The ~~present~~ Senate chamber existing upon the date of adoption of this article shall remain intact until ~~such~~ the election provided for in this section has determined whether the unicameral legislature is to ~~continued~~ continue.

(6) When the provisions of this section have been carried out, it shall be of no further effect.

Section 16. PROHIBITED PAYMENTS. Except for interest on the public debt, ~~N~~no money shall be paid out of the treasury ~~except~~ unless upon an appropriations made by law~~,~~ and ~~on~~ a warrant drawn by the proper officer in pursuance thereof~~, except interest-on-the-public-debt~~

Section 17. CODE OF ETHICS. ~~A-code-of-ethics-for-all state-and-local-officials,-officers,-legislators,-and-state and-local-employees-prohibiting-conflict-between-public-duty and-private-interest-shall-be-described-by-law~~ The legislature shall provide a code of ethics prohibiting conflict between public duty and private interest for senators and all state and local officers and employees.

COMMENTS ON STYLE, FORM, AND GRAMMAR

<u>Section 1.</u> Deletion of unnecessary words does not change substance. The addition of "s" to "power" is self-explanatory.

<u>Section 2.</u> Grammatical changes do not alter substance.

<u>Section 3.</u> Rearrangement does not alter substance.

<u>Section 4.</u> As the second sentence came from the Committe of the Whole, it did not require six months' residence in a multi-county district. Because there did not appear to be a substantive reason for the difference, the drafting change does require such residence. Additions concern districts which may consist of only parts of more than one county.

<u>Section 5.</u> Here and throughout the rest of the Article, the label "senator" was substituted for "member for the legislature," in order that the unicameral and bicameral alternatives might be separate. Other changes do not alter substance. The second sentence of subsection (1) permits a "carryover" senator to fix his own compensation.

<u>Section 6.</u> No change in substance.

<u>Section 8.</u> The provision has been rewritten to accord with the treatment of the elector's privilege in section 6, SUFFRAGE AND ELECTIONS. There is no change in substance.

<u>Section 9.</u> The rewriting attempts to update style, and to avoid repetition of the phrase "under the state," the meaning of which is unclear.

<u>Section 10.</u> Changes to accomplish clarity and brevity do not affect substance. Addition of "for good cause shown" to the last sentence of subsection (1) clarifies the extent of the power.

<u>Section 11.</u> Changes in language and order do not alter substance. The last sentence of subsection (3) becomes

subsection (6).

Section 12 The verb has been changed to make certain the prohibition.

Section 13. The change in verb in subsection (1) makes clear that removal is required. Other changes do not alter substance

Section 14. Line 3 "Commission" was substituted for "committee" because the members are called "commissioners" The language of the proposal in what is now the first sentence of subsection (3) could have been read to require the first commission to report to the session which appointed it The alteration in language seeks to avoid that construction

Section 15 As it came from Committee of the Whole, subsection (3) attempted to amend the constitution without providing a method or the substantive content of the amendment The new subsection (3) supplies those omissions but is not a change in substance Changes in language in other subsections do not alter substance

Sections 16 and 17 Titles were added. Rewriting does not alter substance Both sections will probably be moved to other more appropriate Articles later

BE IT PROPOSED BY THE LEGISLATIVE COMMITTEE

That there be a new Article on the Legislature to read as follows

ARTICLE V

THE LEGISLATURE

Section 1 POWER AND STRUCTURE The legislative power is vested in a legislature consisting of a senate and a house of representatives The people reserve to themselves the powers of initiative and referendum

Section 2 SIZE. The size of the legislature shall be provided by law, but the senate shall not have more than 53 or fewer than 50 members and the house shall not have more than 106 or fewer than 100 members

Section 3 ELECTION AND TERMS A member of the house of representatives shall be elected for a term of two years and a member of the senate for a term of four years each to begin on a date provided by law One-half of the senators shall be elected every two years.

Section 4. QUALIFICATIONS A candidate for the legislature shall be a resident of the state for at least one year next preceding the general election For six months next preceding the general election, he shall be a resident of the county if it contains one or more districts or of the district if it contains all or parts of more than one county

Section 5 COMPENSATION (1) Each member of the legislature shall receive compensation for his services and allowances provided by law No legislature may fix its own compensation

(2) The legislature shall create a salary commission

to recommend compensation for the judiciary and elected members of the legislative and executive departments

Section 6 SESSIONS The legislature shall be a continuous body for two-year periods beginning when newly elected members take office. Any business, bill, or resolution pending at adjournment of a session shall carry over with the same status to any other session of the legislature during the biennium The legislature shall meet at least once a year in regular session of not more than 60 legislative days Any legislature may increase the limit on the length of any subsequent session The legislature may be convened in special sessions by the governor or at the written request of a majority of the members

Section 7 VACANCIES A vacancy in the legislature shall be filled by special election for the unexpired term unless otherwise provided by law.

Section 8 IMMUNITY A member of the legislature is privileged from arrest during attendance at sessions of the legislature and in going to and returning therefrom, unless apprehended in the commission of a felony or a breach of the peace He shall not be questioned in any other place for any speech or debate in the legislature

Section 9 DISQUALIFICATION During the term for which he is elected, a senator or representative shall not hold any civil federal, state, county, or municipal office This prohibition does not apply to a notary public or a member of the militia.

Section 10 ORGANIZATION AND PROCEDURE (1) Each house shall judge the election and qualifications of its members. It may by law vest in the courts the power to try and determine contested elections. Each house shall choose its officers from among its members, keep a journal, and make rules for its proceedings. Each house may expel or punish a member for good cause shown with the concurrence of two-thirds of all its members.

(2) A majority of each house constitutes a quorum. A smaller number may adjourn from day to day and compel attendance of absent members.

(3) The sessions of the legislature and of the committee of the whole, all committee meetings, and all hearings shall be open to the public.

(4) The legislature may establish a legislative council and other interim committees.

(5) Neither house shall, without the consent of the other, adjourn or recess for more than three days or to any place other than that in which the two houses are sitting.

Section 11. BILLS. (1) A law shall be passed by bill which shall not be so altered or amended on its passage through the legislature as to change its original purpose. No bill shall become law except by a vote of the majority of all members present.

(2) Every vote of each member of the legislature on each substantive question in the legislature, in any committee, or in committee of the whole shall be recorded and made public. On final passage, the vote shall be taken by ayes and noes and the names entered on the journal.

(3) Each bill, except general appropriation bills and bills for the codification and general revision of the laws, shall contain only one subject, clearly expressed in its title. If any subject is embraced in any act and is not expressed in

the title, only so much of the act not so expressed is void

(4) A general appropriation bill shall contain only appropriations for the ordinary expenses of the legislative, executive, and judicial departments, for interest on the public debt, and for public schools. Every other appropriation shall be made by a separate bill, containing but one subject

(5) No appropriation shall be made for religious, charitable, industrial, educational, or benevolent purposes to any private individual, private association, or private corporation not under control of the state.

(6) A law may be challenged on the ground of noncompliance with this section only within two years after its effective date

Section 12. LOCAL AND SPECIAL LEGISLATION The legislature shall not pass a special or local act when a general act is, or can be made, applicable

Section 13 IMPEACHMENT. (1) The governor, executive officers, heads of state departments, judicial officers, and such other officers as may be made subject to impeachment by law shall be removed from office upon conviction of impeachment. Other proceedings for removal from public office for cause may be provided by law

(2) The legislature shall provide for the manner, procedure, and causes for removal by impeachment and may select the senate as tribunal

(3) Impeachment shall be brought only by a two-thirds vote of the house. The tribunal hearing the charges shall convict for impeachment only by a vote of two-thirds or more of its members.

(4) Conviction shall extend only to removal from office,

but the party, whether convicted or acquitted, shall also be liable to prosecution according to law

Section 14 DISTRICTING AND APPORTIONMENT (1) The state shall be divided into as many districts as there are members of the house, and each district shall elect one representative Each senate district shall be composed of two adjoining house districts, and shall elect one senator Each district shall consist of compact and contiguous territory All districts shall be as nearly equal in population as is practicable

(2) In the legislative session following ratification of this constitution and thereafter in each session preceding each federal population census, a commission of five citizens, none of whom may be public officials, shall be selected to prepare a plan for redistricting and reapportioning the state into legislative and congressional districts The majority and minority leaders of each house shall each designate one commissioner. Within 20 days after their designation, the four commissioners shall select the fifth member, who shall serve as chairman of the commission. If the four members fail to select the fifth member within the time prescribed, a majority of the supreme court shall select him

(3) The commission shall submit its plan to the legislature at the first regular session after its appointment or after the census figures are available Within 30 days after submission, the legislature shall return the plan to the commission with its recommendations. Within 30 days thereafter the commission shall file its final plan with the secretary of state and it shall become law. The commission is then dissolved

Section 15 PROHIBITED PAYMENTS Except for interest on the public debt, no money shall be paid out of the treasury unless upon an appropriation made by law and a warrant drawn by the proper officer in pursuance thereof

Section 16. CODE OF ETHICS The legislature shall provide a code of ethics prohibiting conflict between public duty and private interest for senators and all state and local officers and employees

BE IT PROPOSED BY THE LEGISLATIVE COMMITTEE:

That there be a new Article on the Legislature to read as follows:

ARTICLE V

THE LEGISLATURE

Section 1. POWER AND STRUCTURE. The legislative power ~~of the state~~ is vested in ~~the~~ a ~~legislative assembly~~ legislature consisting of a senate and a house of representatives. The people reserve to themselves the powers of initiative and referendum.

Section 2. SIZE. The size of the legislature shall be ~~prescribed~~ provided by law, but the senate shall ~~consist of~~ not have more than 53 ~~nor less~~ fewer than 50 members and the house ~~of~~ shall not have more than 106 ~~nor less~~ fewer than 100 members.

Section 3. ELECTION AND TERMS ~~OF MEMBERS~~. A member of the house of representatives shall be elected for a term of two years and a member of the senate for a term of four years each to begin on a date provided by law. One-half of the senators shall be elected every two years. ~~The term of the members shall begin on a date provided by law.~~

Section 4. QUALIFICATIONS. A candidate for the legislature shall be a resident of the state for at least one year next preceding the general election. For six months ~~prior to~~ next preceding the general election, he ~~must~~ shall be a resident of the county ~~which~~ if it contains one or more districts ~~and where a~~ or of the district if it ~~consists~~ contains all or parts of more than one county~~, he must reside within that district.~~

Section 5 COMPENSATION (1) Each member of the legislature shall receive compensation for his services and allowances ~~as-may-be-prescribed~~ provided by law No legislature may fix its own compensation

(2) The legislature shall create ~~A~~ a salary commission ~~shall-be-created-by-the-legislature~~ to recommend compensation for the judiciary and elected members of the legislative and executive ~~and-judicial-compensation.~~ departments

Section 6 SESSIONS The legislature shall be a continuous body for two-year periods beginning ~~on-the-date~~ when newly elected members take office Any business, bill, or resolution pending at adjournment of a session shall carry over with the same status to any ~~further~~ other session of the legislature during the biennium The legislature shall meet at least once a year in regular sessions of not more than 60 legislative days ~~or-less~~ Any legislature may increase the limit on the length of any subsequent session The legislature may be convened in special sessions by the governor, or at the written request of a majority of the members

Section 7 VACANCIES A vacancy in the legislature shall be filled by special election for the unexpired term unless otherwise provided by law

Section 8 IMMUNITY ~~The-members-of-the-legislature-shall,-in-all-cases,-except-felony-and-breach-of-the-peace,-be-privileged-from-arrest-during-their-attendance-at-the-sessions-of-the-legislature,-and-in-going-to-and-returning-from-the-same,-and-for-any-speech-or-debate-in-the-legislature,-they-shall-not-be-questioned-in-any-other-place.~~ A member of the legislature is privileged from arrest during attendance at sessions of the legislature and in going to and returning therefrom, unless apprehended in the commission of a felony or a breach of the peace. He shall not be questioned in any other place for any speech or debate in the legislature.

Section 9. DISQUALIFICATION. ~~No senator or representative shall, during the term for which he shall have been elected, be appointed to any civil office under the state, and no member of congress, or other person holding an office (except notary public, or in the militia) under the United States or this state, shall be a member of either house during his continuance in office.~~ During the term for which he is elected, a senator or representative shall not hold any civil federal, state, county, or municipal office. This prohibition does not apply to a notary public or a member of the militia.

Section 10. ORGANIZATION AND PROCEDURE. (1) Each house shall judge the election and qualifications of its members. ~~and~~ It may by law vest in the courts the ~~trial and determination of~~ power to try and determine contested elections ~~of its members~~. Each house shall choose its officers from among its members~~;~~, keep a journal~~;~~, and make rules for its proceedings~~;~~. ~~and~~ Each house may expel or punish a member for good cause shown with the concurrence of two-thirds of all its members.

(2) A majority of each house constitutes a quorum ~~to do business~~. A smaller number may adjourn from day to day and compel attendance of absent members.

(3) The sessions of the legislature~~,~~ and of the committee of the whole, ~~and~~ all committee meetings, and all hearings shall be open to the public.

(4) ~~There-may-be-a-legislative-council-and-t~~The legislature may establish a legislative council and other interim committees

(5) Neither house shall, without the consent of the other, adjourn or recess for more than three days~~,~~ ~~nor~~ to any ~~other~~ place other than that in which the two houses ~~shall-be~~ are sitting

Section 11 BILLS (1) A law shall be passed by bill~~,~~ ~~and-a-bill~~ which shall not be so altered or amended on its passage through the legislature as to change its original purpose No bill shall become law except by a vote of the majority of all members present.

(2) ~~The-vote-of-each-member-of-the-legislature-and its-committees-on-any-substantive-question-shall-be-recorded and-made-public-~~ Every vote of each member of the legislature on each substantive question in the legislature, in any committee, or in committee of the whole shall be recorded and made public

~~(3)--No-bill-shall-become-law-except-by-a-vote-of-the-majority-of-all-members-present,-and~~ ~~o~~On final passage, the vote shall be taken by ayes and noes and the names entered on the journal.

~~(4)~~ (3) Each bill, except general appropriation bills~~,~~ and bills for the codification and general revision of the laws, shall contain only one subject, ~~which-shall-be~~ clearly expressed in its title~~,~~ ~~but~~ ~~i~~If any subject ~~shall-be~~ is embraced in any act ~~which-shall~~ and is not ~~be~~ expressed in the title, ~~such-act shall-be-void~~ only ~~as-to~~ so much ~~thereof-as-shall~~ of the act not be so expressed is void ~~A-law-may-be-challenged-on-the grounds-of-non-compliance-with-this-section-within-two-years~~

~~after-its-effective-date-but-not-after-that-period-~~

~~(5)~~ (4) A ~~G~~general appropriation bills shall contain only appropriations for the ordinary expenses of the legislative, executive, and judicial departments ~~of-the-state~~, for interest on the public debt, and for public schools ~~All~~ Every other appropriations shall be made by a separate bills~~,~~ ~~each~~ containing but one subject

~~(6)~~ (5) No appropriation shall be made for religious, charitable, industrial, educational, or benevolent purposes to any private individual, private association, or private corporation not under control of the state

(6) A law may be challenged on the ground of non-compliance with this section only within two years after its effective date.

Section 12. LOCAL AND SPECIAL LEGISLATION The legislature ~~may~~ shall not pass a special or local act when a general act is, or can be made, applicable.

Section 13. IMPEACHMENT (1) The governor, executive officers, heads of state departments, judicial officers, and such other officers as may be made subject to impeachment by law ~~may~~ shall be removed from office upon conviction of impeachment Other proceedings for removal from public office for cause may be provided by law

(2) The legislature shall provide for the manner, procedure, and causes for removal by impeachment and may select the senate as tribunal.

(3) Impeachment ~~can~~ shall be brought only by a two-thirds vote of the house. ~~and-no-conviction~~ The tribunal hearing the charges shall convict for impeachment ~~shall-be-made-except~~ only by a vote of two-thirds or more of ~~the~~ its members ~~of-the-tribunal-hearing-the-charges~~

(4) ~~Such-c~~Conviction shall ~~only~~ extend only to removal from office, but the party, whether convicted or acquitted, shall also be liable to prosecution according to law

Section 14. DISTRICTING AND APPORTIONMENT (1) The state shall be divided into as many ~~house~~ districts as there are ~~representatives~~ members of the house, and each district shall elect one representative Each senate district shall be ~~comprised~~ composed of two adjoining ~~representative~~ house districts,~~for-the-election-of~~ and shall elect one senator ~~Every~~ Each ~~legislative~~ district shall consist of compact and contiguous territory_ ~~and~~ All districts shall be ~~so~~ as nearly equal in population as is practicable.

(2) In the legislative session following ratification of this constitution and thereafter in ~~the~~ each session preceding each federal population census ~~made-by-the-authority-of-the United-States~~, a ~~committee~~ commission of five citizens, none of whom may be public officials, shall be ~~designated~~-selected to ~~draft~~ prepare a plan for redistricting and reapportioning the state into legislative and congressional districts. The majority and minority leaders of each house shall each designate ~~a~~ one commissioner ~~The-four-commissioners,-w~~Within 20 days after their designation, the four commissioners shall select the fifth member, who shall serve as chairman of the commission If the four members fail to select the fifth member within the time prescribed, a majority of the supreme court shall ~~appoint the-chairman~~ select him

(3) The ~~appointed~~ commission shall ~~draw-up-a-plan-for reapportioning-and-redistricting-legislative-and-congressional districts-and~~ submit ~~this~~ its plan to the legislature at the first regular session after ~~ratification-of-this-constitution~~

its appointment or after the census figures are available. Within ~~(30) thirty~~ days after the submission, ~~to it~~ the legislature shall return the plan to the commission with its recommendations ~~for change and the commission shall w~~Within ~~(30) thirty~~ days thereafter the commission shall file ~~with the Secretary of State its~~ final plan with the secretary of state and ~~the same~~ it shall become law. ~~After enactment of a valid plan this~~ The commission ~~shall be~~ is then dissolved.

Section 15 PROHIBITED PAYMENTS Except for interest on the public debt, ~~N~~no money shall be paid out of the treasury ~~except~~ unless upon an appropriation~~s~~ made by law~~,~~ and ~~on~~ a warrant drawn by the proper officer in pursuance thereof~~, except interest on the public debt~~.

Section 16 CODE OF ETHICS ~~A code of ethics for all state and local officials, officers, legislators, and state and local employees prohibiting conflict between public duty and private interest shall be described by law.~~ The legislature shall provide a code of ethics prohibiting conflict between public duty and private interest for senators and all state and local officers and employees

Report No 3 - Legislative - (Bicameral)

COMMENTS ON STYLE, FORM, AND GRAMMAR

NB - Only comments which differ from those applied to the UNICAMERAL proposal appear here.

Sections 1, 2, 3, 10, 13, and 14 Grammatical changes do not alter substance

(UNICAMERAL)

ORDER OF BUSINESS NO. 5 - FINAL CONSIDERATION

STYLE AND DRAFTING - LEGISLATIVE - NO. III

ARTICLE ____

THE LEGISLATURE

Section 1. POWER AND STRUCTURE. The legislative power is vested in a legislature of one chamber whose members are designated senators. The people reserve to themselves the powers of initiative and referendum.

Section 2. SIZE. The number of senators shall be provided by law, but it shall not be smaller than 90 nor larger than 105.

Section 3. ELECTION AND TERMS. A senator shall be elected for a term of four years to begin on a date provided by law. One-half of the senators shall be elected every two years.

Section 4. QUALIFICATIONS. A candidate for the legislature shall be a resident of the state for at least one year next preceding the general election. For six months next preceding the general election, he shall be a resident of the county if it contains one or more districts or of the district if it contains all or parts of more than one county.

Section 5. COMPENSATION. (1) Each member of the legislature shall receive compensation for his services and allowances provided by law. No legislature may fix its own compensation.

(2) The legislature shall create a salary commission to recommend compensation for the judiciary and elected members of the legislative and executive departments.

Section 6. SESSIONS. The legislature shall be a

continuous body for two-year periods beginning when newly elected members take office. Any business, bill, or resolution pending at adjournment of a session shall carry over with the same status to any other session of the legislature during the biennium. The legislature shall meet at least once a year in regular sessions of not more than 60 legislative days. Any legislature may increase the limit on the length of any subsequent session. The legislature may be convened in special sessions by the governor or at the written request of a majority of the members.

Section 7. VACANCIES. A vacancy in the legislature shall be filled by special election for the unexpired term unless otherwise provided by law.

Section 8. IMMUNITY. A member of the legislature is privileged from arrest during attendance at sessions of the legislature and in going to and returning therefrom, unless apprehended in the commission of a felony or a breach of the peace. He shall not be questioned in any other place for any speech or debate in the legislature.

Section 9. DISQUALIFICATION. No member of the legislature shall, during the term for which he shall have been elected, be appointed to any civil office under the state,; and no member of congress, or other person holding an office (except notary public, or in the militia) under the United States or this state, shall be a member of the legislature during his continuance in office.

Section 10. ORGANIZATION AND PROCEDURE. (1) The legislature shall judge the election and qualifications of senators. It may vest by law in the courts the power to try and determine contested elections. It shall choose it officers from among its members, keep a journal, and make rules for its proceedings It may expel or punish a senator for good cause shown with the concurrence of two-thirds of all the senators.

(2) A majority of the senators constitutes a quorum. A smaller number may adjourn from day to day and compel attendance of absent members.

(3) The sessions of the legislature and of the committee of the whole, all committee meetings, and all hearings shall be open to the public

(4) The legislature may establish a legislative council and other interim committees.

Section 11. BILLS. (1) A law shall be passed by bill which shall not be so altered or amended on its passage through the legislature as to change its original purpose. No bill shall become law except by a vote of the majority of all members present and voting

(2) Every vote of each member on each substantive question in the legislature, in any committee, or in committee of the whole shall be recorded and made public. On final passage, the vote shall be taken by ayes and noes and the names entered on the journal.

(3) Each bill, except general appropriation bills and bills for the codification and general revision of the laws, shall contain only one subject, clearly expressed in its title. If any subject is embraced in any act and is not expressed in the title, only so much of the act not so expressed is void.

(4) A general appropriation bill shall contain only appropriations for the ordinary expenses of the legislative, executive, and judicial departments, for interest on the public

debt, and for public schools. Every other appropriation shall be made by a separate bill containing but one subject

(5) No appropriation shall be made for religious, charitable, industrial, educational, or benevolent purposes to any private individual, private association, or private corporation not under control of the state.

(6) A law may be challenged on the ground of noncompliance with this section only within two years after its effective date.

Section 12. LOCAL AND SPECIAL LEGISLATION. The legislature shall not pass a special or local act when a general act is, or can be made, applicable.

Section 13. IMPEACHMENT. (1) The governor, executive officers, heads of state departments, judicial officers, and such other officers as may be provided by law are subject to impeachment, and upon conviction shall be removed from office Other proceedings for removal from public office for cause may be provided by law

(2) The legislature shall provide for the manner, procedure, and causes for impeachment and shall provide for a tribunal.

(3) Impeachment can be brought only by a two-thirds vote of the legislature The tribunal hearing the charges shall convict only by a vote of two-thirds or more of its members

(4) Conviction shall extend only to removal from office, but the party, whether convicted or acquitted, shall also be liable to prosecution according to law.

Section 14 DISTRICTING AND APPORTIONMENT (1) Tthe state shall be divided into as many districts as there are senators and each district shall elect one senator. Each district shall consist of compact and contiguous territory. All districts shall be as nearly equal in population as is practicable

(2) In the legislative session following ratification of this constitution and thereafter in each session preceding each federal population census, a commission of five citizens, none of whom may be public officials, shall be selected to prepare a plan for redistricting and reapportioning the state into legislative and congressional districts The majority and minority leaders of the legislature shall each select two commissioners Within 20 days after their designation, the four commissioners shall select the fifth member, who shall serve as chairman of the commission If the four members fail to select the fifth member within the time provided, a majority of the supreme court shall select him.

(3) The commission shall submit its plan to the legislature at the first regular session after its appointment or after the census figures are available Within 30 days after submission, the legislature shall return the plan to the commission with its recommendations Within 30 days thereafter, the commission shall file its final plan with the secretary of state and it shall become law The commission is then dissolved.

Section 15. REFERENDUM OF UNICAMERAL LEGISLATURE (1) In 1980 the secretary of state shall place upon the ballot at the general election the question "Shall the unicameral legislature form be continued?"

(2) If a majority of the qualified electors voting on the question answer in the affirmative, the form shall be

continued, and this section shall be of no further effect

(3) If a majority of the qualified electors voting on the question answer in the negative, Article ____ of this Constitution is amended by deleting sections 1, 2, 3, 10, 13, and 14, and inserting in lieu thereof the following

(a) "Section 1. POWER AND STRUCTURE The legislative power is vested in a legislature consisting of a senate and a house of representatives The people reserve to themselves the powers of initiative and referendum "

(b) "Section 2. SIZE The size of the legislature shall be provided by law, but the senate shall not have more than ~~53~~ 50 or fewer than ~~50~~ 40 members and the house shall not have more than ~~106~~ 100 or fewer than ~~100~~ 80 members "

(c) "Section 3. ELECTION AND TERMS A member of the house of representatives shall be elected for a term of two years and a member of the senate for a term of four years, each to begin on a date provided by law One-half of the senators shall be elected every two years."

(d) "Section 10 ORGANIZATION AND PROCEDURE. (1) Each house shall judge the election and qualifications of its members It may by law vest in the courts the power to try and determine contested elections. Each house shall choose its officers from among its members, keep a journal, and make rules for its proceedings Each house may expel or punish a member for good cause shown with the concurrence of two-thirds of all its members

"(2) A majority of each house constitutes a quorum A smaller number may adjourn from day to day and compel attendance of absent members

"(3) The sessions of the legislature and of the committee

of the whole, all committee meetings, and all hearings shall be open to the public.

"(4) The legislature may establish a legislative council and other interim committees

"(5) Neither house shall, without the consent of the other, adjourn or recess for more than three days or to any place other than that in which the two houses are sitting "

(e) "Section 13. IMPEACHMENT. (1) The governor, executive officers, heads of state departments, judicial officers, and such other officers as may be ~~made subject~~ provided by law are subject to impeachment, and upon conviction shall be removed from office ~~upon conviction of impeachment~~ Other proceedings for removal from public office for cause may be provided by law

"(2) The legislature shall provide for the manner, procedure and causes for ~~removal by~~ impeachment and may select the senate as tribunal

"(3) Impeachment shall be brought only by a two-thirds vote of the house The tribunal hearing the charges shall convict only by a vote of two-thirds or more of its members.

"(4) Conviction shall extend only to removal from office, but the party, whether convicted or acquitted, shall also be liable to prosecution according to law."

(f) "Section 14. DISTRICTING AND APPORTIONMENT. (1) The state shall be divided into as many districts as there are members of the house, and each district shall elect one representative. Each senate district shall be composed of two adjoining house districts, and shall elect one senator. Each district shall consist of compact and contiguous territory. All districts shall be as nearly equal in population as is practicable.

"(2) In the legislative session following this amendment and thereafter in each session preceding each federal population census, a commission of five citizens, none of whom may be public officials, shall be selected to prepare a plan for redistricting and reapportioning the state into legislative and congressional districts. The majority and minority leaders of each house shall each designate one commissioner. Within 20 days after their designation, the four commissioners shall select the fifth member, who shall serve as chairman of the commission. If the four members fail to select the fifth member within the time provided, a majority of the supreme court shall select him.

"(3) The commission shall submit its plan to the legislature at the first regular session after its appointment or after the census figures are available. Within 30 days after submission, the legislature shall return the plan to the commission with its recommendations. Within 30 days thereafter, the commission shall file its final plan with the secretary of state and it shall become law. The commission is then dissolved."

(4) The members of the unicameral legislature shall remain in office and their authority to act shall continue until the members of a bicameral body are elected and qualified.

(5) The Senate chamber existing upon the date of adoption of this Article shall remain intact until the election provided for in this section has determined whether the unicameral legislature is to continue.

(6) When the provisions of this section have been carried out, it shall be of no further effect.

Section 16. PROHIBITED PAYMENTS. Except for interest on the public debt, no money shall be paid out of the treasury unless upon an appropriation made by law and a warrant drawn by the proper officer in pursuance thereof.

Section 17. CODE OF ETHICS. The legislature shall provide a code of ethics prohibiting conflict between public duty and private interest for members and all state and local officers and employees.

(BICAMERAL)

ORDER OF BUSINESS NO 5-FINAL CONSIDERATION

STYLE AND DRAFTING-LEGISLATIVE-NO III

ARTICLE __

THE LEGISLATURE

Section 1. POWER AND STRUCTURE. The legislative power is vested in a legislature consisting of a senate and a house of representatives. The people reserve to themselves the powers of initiative and referendum.

Section 2. SIZE. The size of the legislature shall be provided by law, but the senate shall not have more than 50 or fewer than 40 members and the house shall not have more than 100 or fewer than 80 members.

Section 3. ELECTION AND TERMS. A member of the house of representatives shall be elected for a term of two years and a member of the senate for a term of four years each to begin on a date provided by law. One-half of the senators shall be elected every two years.

Section 4. QUALIFICATIONS. A candidate for the legislature shall be a resident of the state for at least one year next preceding the general election. For six months next preceding the general election, he shall be a resident of the county if it contains one or more districts or of the district if it contains all or parts of more than one county.

Section 5. COMPENSATION. (1) Each member of the legislature shall receive compensation for his services and allowances provided by law. No legislature may fix its own compensation.

(2) The legislature shall create a salary commission

to recommend compensation for the judiciary and elected members of the legislative and executive departments.

Section 6. SESSIONS. The legislature shall be a continuous body for two-year periods beginning when newly elected members take office. Any business, bill, or resolution pending at adjournment of a session shall carry over with the same status to any other session of the legislature during the biennium. The legislature shall meet at least once a year in regular session of not more than 60 legislative days. Any legislature may increase the limit on the length of any subsequent session The legislature may be convened in special sessions by the governor or at the written request of a majority of the members.

Section 7. VACANCIES. A vacancy in the legislature shall be filled by special election for the unexpired term unless otherwise provided by law.

Section 8. IMMUNITY. A member of the legislature is privileged from arrest during attendance at sessions of the legislature and in going to and returning therefrom, unless apprehended in the commission of a felony or a breach of the peace He shall not be questioned in any other place for any speech or debate in the legislature.

Section 9. DISQUALIFICATION. No **senator-or-representa-tive** member of the legislature shall, during the term for which he shall have been elected, be appointed to any civil office under the state, and no member of congress, or other person holding an office (except notary public, or in the militia) under the United States or this state, shall be a member of **either house** the legislature during his continuance in office.

Section 10. ORGANIZATION AND PROCEDURE. (1) Each house shall judge the election and qualifications of its members. It may by law vest in the courts the power to try and determine contested elections. Each house shall choose its officers from among its members, keep a journal, and make rules for its proceedings. Each house may expel or punish a member for good cause shown with the concurrence of two-thirds of all its members.

(2) A majority of each house constitutes a quorum. A smaller number may adjourn from day to day and compel attendance of absent members.

(3) The sessions of the legislature and of the committee of the whole, all committee meetings, and all hearings shall be open to the public.

(4) The legislature may establish a legislative council and other interim committees.

(5) Neither house shall, without the consent of the other, adjourn or recess for more than three days or to any place other than that in which the two houses are sitting.

Section 11. BILLS. (1) A law shall be passed by bill which shall not be so altered or amended on its passage through the legislature as to change its original purpose. No bill shall become law except by a vote of the majority of all members present and voting.

(2) Every vote of each member of the legislature on each substantive question in the legislature, in any committee, or in committee of the whole shall be recorded and made public. On final passage, the vote shall be taken by ayes and noes and the names entered on the journal.

(3) Each bill, except general appropriation bills and

CPSIA information can be obtained at www.ICGtesting.com
Printed in the USA
LVOW09s1327080216

474180LV00014B/348/P

9 781293 84640